D1716973

Exploring ARGENTINA

with the FIVE Themes of Geography

by Jane Holiday

The Rosen Publishing Group's
PowerKids Press™
New York

Published in 2005 by The Rosen Publishing Group, Inc.
29 East 21st Street, New York, NY 10010

First Edition

Editor: Geeta Sobha
Book Design: Michelle Innes

Photo Credits: Cover, p. 1 © Royalty-Free/Corbis; p. 9 © Hubert Stadler/Corbis; p. 10 © Francesc Muntada/Corbis; p. 10 (rheas) © Wolfgang Kaehler/Corbis; pp. 12, 15 © Sergio Pitamitz/Corbis; p. 12 (gaucho) © Pablo Corral Vega/Corbis; p. 13 © Corbis; p. 15 (Rio Gallegos) © Neil Beer/Corbis; p. 16 © Walter Bibikow/Getty Images; p. 16 © (sheep) Geoffrey Clifford/Getty Images; p. 16 (guanacos) © Kit Kittle/Corbis; p. 19 © Peter Johnson/Corbis; p. 19 (Ushuaia) © Bob Krist/Corbis; p. 21 (top) © Phillip and Karen Smith/Getty Images; p. 21 (bottom) © S.P. Gillette/Corbis

Library of Congress Cataloging-in-Publication Data

Holiday, Jane.
     Exploring Argentina with the five themes of geography / by Jane
     Holiday—1st ed.
     p. cm. — (The library of the Western Hemisphere)
     Includes index.
     Summary: Briefly looks at Argentina's geography in terms of five
     geographical themes: location; place, or physical characteristics;
     human-environment interaction; movement, or transportation; and region.
     ISBN 1-4042-2678-8 (lib. bdg.) — ISBN 0-8239-4638-X (pbk.)
     1. Argentina—Geography—Juvenile literature. [1.
     Argentina—Geography.] I. Title. II. Series.

     F2810.9.H65 2005
     918.2—dc22

                                                    2003018553

Manufactured in the United States of America

Contents

The FIVE Themes of Geography

Geography is the study of Earth, including its people, resources, climate, and physical features. When we study a particular country or area, such as Argentina, we use the five themes of geography: location, place, human-environment interaction, movement, and regions. These themes help us organize and understand important information about the geography of places all over the world. Let's use the five themes to help us learn about Argentina.

1 Location

Where is Argentina?

You can define where Argentina is by its absolute, or exact, location and also by its relative, or general, location. Absolute location tells exactly where a place is in the world. We use the imaginary lines of longitude and latitude to give a place its absolute location.

Relative location tells where a place is by showing other places near it. Also, relative location can be a place's cardinal point. Cardinal points are east, west, north, and south.

2 Place

What is Argentina like?

To know Argentina, we must study its physical and human features. The physical features include landforms, natural resources, bodies of water, climate, and plant and animal life. Human features include cities, buildings, government, and traditions, that have been created by people.

3 Human-Environment Interaction

How do the people and the environment of Argentina affect each other?

Human-environment interaction explains how the land has affected the way people in Argentina live. It also explains how the people of Argentina have changed their environment or adapted to it.

4 Movement

How do people, goods, and ideas get from place to place in Argentina?

This theme explains how products, people, and ideas move around this vast country. Also, it shows how they move from Argentina to other countries in the world.

5 Regions

What does Argentina have in common with other places around the world? What features do places within Argentina share to make them part of a region?

Places are grouped into regions by physical and cultural features that they share. We'll look at features that Argentina shares with other areas, making it part of certain regions. We'll also look at regions within Argentina.

Argentina's absolute location is 34° south and 64° west. We can find Argentina's relative location by looking at the places that surround it. Argentina is bordered by five countries: Bolivia, Brazil, Chile, Paraguay, and Uruguay. It is also bordered on its eastern coast by the Atlantic Ocean.

Argentina stretches from the center of South America down to the tip of the continent. It covers most of the southern portion of South America. No wonder Argentina is sometimes called the tail of South America!

Where in the World?

Absolute location is the point where the lines of longitude and latitude meet.

Longitude tells a place's position in degrees east or west of the prime meridian, a line that runs through Greenwich, London.

Latitude tells a place's position in degrees north or south of the equator, the imaginary line that goes around the middle of the earth.

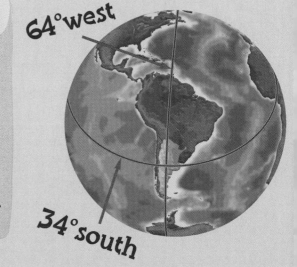

64°west

34°south

Physical Features

Many different kinds of land can be found in Argentina, from flat plains to tall mountains. The Andes mountain range runs along the western border of Argentina. The flat, grassy plains, known as the Pampa, cover the central part of Argentina, from the Atlantic Ocean to the Andes Mountains. In southern Argentina is Patagonia, home to beautiful mountains, forests, lakes, waterfalls, and beaches. It also has deep canyons, windy flatlands, and cool deserts.

Most of Argentina has a temperate climate—the summers are not very hot, and the winters are not very cold. However, high up in the Andes and down at the southern tip of Patagonia, the weather can be cold and harsh. In northern Argentina, the weather can be hot and humid.

Salt plains can be found in Salinas Grandes in Jujuy. Jujuy is in northwestern Argentina.

Mount Aconcagua in northwestern Argentina is the highest mountain in the Western Hemisphere. It is part of the Andes mountain range.

9

Rheas are large, flightless birds that are found in the pampas of Argentina and Brazil.

Los Glaciares National Park is in Patagonia. In the east, the park is made up of forests and grassy plains. In the west, there are lakes, glaciers, and snowfields.

Argentina is home to many different kinds of wildlife. In Patagonia, there are penguins, sea lions, and elephant seals. Birds in the tropical regions include flamingos and parrots. Giant condors patrol the skies in the Andes Mountains. Anteaters, jaguars, wild horses, and even miniature donkeys make their home on the Pampa.

Human Features

Over 38 million people live in Argentina. Most people live in cities or large towns. About one-third of the people live in and around the country's capital, Buenos Aires. Most of the major businesses can be found in and around the big cities.

Argentina's congress hall is located in Buenos Aires. Senators are voted into Congress to represent the provinces.

The government of Argentina is a republic. In a republic, the people elect a president, a vice president, and a congress.

Argentina's culture has strong Spanish and Italian influences. The official language of Argentina is Spanish. European-style architecture can be found in cities and towns across the country.

Two important parts of Argentinean culture are the gauchos and the tango. Gauchos were cowboys who are seen as brave and hardworking. The tango is a style of dance and music.

Gauchos lived and worked on the prairies of Argentina from the mid-18th to the mid-19th centuries. They were mainly mestizos, which means they were descended from both Indian and Spanish peoples.

Argentina's weather and land influence where people live. In the Andes and most of Patagonia, extremely cold weather make living there difficult. Because of poor soil and extremely hot weather, few people live in the Gran Chaco, which is in northwestern Argentina.

In the Pampa, there can be fierce winds and thunderstorms. The floods that follow these storms can do tremendous damage. However, the Pampa as well as Mesopotamia, in the north, is Argentina's most populated region. The rich soil of these areas allows for farming and cattle raising.

Argentineans depend on their natural resources to meet their needs. Petroleum, a form of oil, and coal are used for energy. Several enormous dams have been built on rivers and lakes to provide hydroelectricity to the country. Also, Argentinean farmers depend on the rivers

Rio Gallegos is the capital of Santa Cruz, a province of Argentina. It is known for oil production and sheep breeding.

Argentinean farmers take advantage of the rich soil in the Jujuy to grow sugarcane and other crops.

15

In Patagonia, sheep farms have threatened wildlife such as the guanaco. Farmers feel that these animals take over areas where sheep graze.

The number of automobiles in Buenos Aires is about 60 percent of all the cars in Argentina. Toxic chemicals released by cars cause dangerous air pollution.

to provide irrigation and fertile soil for farming. Many people work in the fishing industries as well.

In Argentina, as everywhere else, environmental problems are the result of human activity. This is especially true around the major cities, such as Buenos Aires. Air pollution from cars and water pollution from factories are harming the environment.

About half of the land in Argentina is used for farming and raising animals. To increase their beef supply, ranchers have taken more land on which to graze their cattle. This has destroyed grasslands in the north. In the south, sheep farming also poses a threat to natural habitats.

Argentina is working hard to keep its environment safe. The government has created national parks to preserve wildlife. It has also signed agreements with other countries to protect the environment.

4 Movement

Argentineans depend on transportation routes to help move people and goods across their vast country. All major routes lead in and out of Buenos Aires. National and international airlines fly in and out of the 1,369 airports.

Argentina's waterways play an important role in transportation too. Ports and harbors in cities such as Bahia Blanca and La Plata allow travel and shipping of goods. Tunnels and bridges connect Argentina with other countries in South America.

News and ideas travel in many ways across Argentina and to the rest of the world. There are 42 major TV stations. Argentina's newspapers, such as *La Prensa*, are among the most respected in Latin America. Argentina's writers, such as Jorge Luis Borges, have found worldwide success.

Ushuaia is an important port on the Beagle Canal on Ushuaia Bay. The town was settled in the 1870s by the British. It is the world's southernmost city.

Argentina's total roadway measurement is the third largest in South America. This highway is across marshes near Goya.

5 Regions

Argentina is part of a cultural region called Latin America, where most people speak a Romance language, such as Spanish, Portuguese, or French. Latin America is made up of countries in the Western Hemisphere, south of the United States.

Since most of Argentina has temperate weather, it is considered part of the temperate region of the Southern Hemisphere.

Within Argentina there are different types of physical regions. The Pampa, where Argentina's crops are grown, is considered Argentina's agricultural region. The Gran Chaco is mostly made up of forests. Mesopotamia, located between the Uruguay and Paraguay Rivers, is mostly grassy plains and swamps.

Argentina is divided into 23 provinces, which are regions ruled by the government.

Argentina's geographical regions include the Gran Chaco, the Pampa, Patagonia, Mesopotamia, and the Andes.

Andes

Gran Chaco

Mesopotamia

Pampa

Andes

Patagonia

Modern-day gauchos raise sheep along with cattle on the Pampa.

In parts of Patagonia, the average temperature is 32°F (0°C).

Argentina's Flag

Population (2003) 38,740,807

Language Spanish

Absolute location 34° south, 64° west

Capital city Buenos Aires

Area 1,068,296 square miles (2,766,890 square kilometers)

Highest point Cerro Aconcagua 22,834.646 feet (6,960 meters)

Lowest point Salinas Chicas (on Peninsula Valdes) -131.234 feet (-40m)

Land boundaries Bolivia, Brazil, Chile, Paraguay, Uruguay

Natural resources grasslands, timber, lead, zinc, tin, copper, iron ore, manganese, petroleum, uranium, natural gas

Agricultural products sunflower seeds, lemons, soybeans, grapes, corn, tobacco, peanuts, tea, wheat, livestock

Major exports cereals, oilseeds, meat, wool, hides, dairy products, transportation equipment, and forest products (notably tannin and tung oil)

Major imports machinery and electrical equipment; iron, iron manufactures, and other metals; chemicals; mineral fuels and oils; and paper and food products

Glossary

architecture (AR-ki-tek-chur) The style in which buildings are designed.

culture (KUHL-chur) The way of life, ideas, customs, and traditions shared by a group of people.

hemisphere (HEM-uhss-fihr) One half of the earth.

hydroelectricity (hye-droh-i-lek-TRISS-uh-tee) Electricity produced by water power that turns a generator.

interaction (in-tur-AK-shuhn) The action between people, groups, or things.

irrigation (ihr-uh-GAY-shuhn) When water is applied to crops by using channels and pipes.

pampa (PAM-puh) A grass-covered plain in South America.

province (PROV-uhnss) A district or region of some countries.

region (REE-juhn) An area or a district.

republic (ri-PUHB-lik) A form of government in which the people have the power to elect representatives who manage the government.

resource (ri-SORSS) Something that is valuable or useful to a place or person.

temperate (TEM-pur-it) Climate that does not have very high or very low temperatures.

Index

Web Sites

Due to the changing nature of Internet links, PowerKids Press has developed an online list of Web sites related to the subject of this book. This site is updated regularly. Please use this link to access the list:
http://www.powerkidslinks.com/lwh/argent